HAR

DLY

WAR

DON MEE CHOI

Wave Books

Seattle and New York

PUBLISHED BY WAVE BOOKS

WWW.WAVEPOETRY.COM

WAVE BOOKS TITLES ARE DISTRIBUTED TO THE TRADE BY

CONSORTIUM BOOK SALES AND DISTRIBUTION

PHONE: 800-283-3572 / SAN 631-760X

LIBRARY OF CONGRESS CATALOGING-IN-PUBLICATION DATA

CHOI, DON MEE.

[POEMS. SELECTIONS]

HARDLY WAR / DON MEE CHOI.

PAGES ; CM

ISBN 978-1-940696-23-2 (LIMITED EDITION HARDCOVER) —

ISBN 978-1-940696-21-8 (SOFTCOVER)

I. TITLE.

PS3603.H65A6 2016

811'.6—DC23

2015025698

DESIGNED AND COMPOSED BY QUEMADURA

PRINTED IN THE UNITED STATES OF AMERICA

9 8 7 6 5 4 3

WAVE BOOKS 054

''PLEASE!''/SMOKEY THE BEAR POSTER

APPEARS COURTESY OF THE VIETNAM CENTER

AND ARCHIVE AT TEXAS TECH UNIVERSITY.

It is funny about wars, they ought to be different but they are not.

GERTRUDE STEIN, *Wars I Have Seen* (1945)

The Photograph then becomes a bizarre *medium*, a new form of hallucination: false on the level of perception, true on the level of time: a temporal hallucination, so to speak, a modest, *shared* hallucination (on the one hand "it is not there," on the other "but it has indeed been"): a mad image, chafed by reality.

ROLAND BARTHES, *Camera Lucida*, trans. Richard Howard (1981)

Her father filmed the carpet-fucking-bombing in Cambodia.

C. D. WRIGHT (2014)

FOR MY FATHER

Hardly War

Purely Illustrative

Hardly Opera

HARDLY

WAR

RACE = NATION

I was born in a tiny, traditional, tile-roofed house, a house my father bought with award money he received for his photographs of the April 19, 1960 Revolution. The student-led revolution overthrew the authoritarian South Korean president, Syngman Rhee, installed by the US government in 1948. He tells me even elementary school students came out to join high school and college students in protest, their arms locked shoulder to shoulder. And what he cannot forget are the shoeshine boys, Korean War orphans who eked out a living on the streets of Seoul. Many of them gave up their lives in the uprising. Police opened fire, killing about 180 and wounding thousands. In 1972, the height of the US-backed dictatorship under Park Chung Hee, we bade farewell to the house I was born in. Even after several decades of living outside of South Korea, this is the house I still return to. It is my psychic and linguistic base, a site of perpetual farewell and return, a site of my political act—translation and writing.

My early education in South Korea trained me to think of race as nation and of nation as race, hence race=nation. A Korean term, *uri minjok*—our race, our national identity—was imagined, a crucial construction and a mobilizing force in the anti-colonial, independence movement during the Japanese occupation, 1910–45. When Korea fell under the control of the US military government in 1945, a part of our race had split off as *ppalgaengi*, Reds or Commies. But really, anyone in "those white pajama things," traditional pants, which the majority of the Koreans wore back then, was seen as a gook. This is how a gook=nation was born. Our race, our national identity, even our clothing became racialized and geopoliticized within the

3

global class war. Therefore, when I was born in the tiny, tile-roofed house, I was already geopolitically raced. Hence, me=gook.

While I was growing up in Hong Kong, I saw more of my father's photographs than of my father because he was always away in various war zones. He would bring back photographs of the wars he saw, then leave again. He also left us a map, a wall-sized map of Southeast Asia, framed and hung above our dining table, so we could track him across Vietnam, Cambodia, and Laos. What I am attempting to do with my poems and my father's photographs is what I used to do as a child when I stared at my father's photographs and maps. I'm trying to imagine race=nation, its language, its wars. I am trying to fold race into geopolitics and geopolitics into poetry. Hence, geopolitical poetics. It involves disobeying history, severing its ties to power. It strings together the faintly remembered, the faintly imagined, the faintly discarded, which is to say race=nation gets to speak its own faint history in its own faint language. Its mere umbilical cord is hardly attached to anything at all. Hence, hardly=war.

A LITTLE GLOSSARY

미=국 수=국 무=국 화=국 애=국

Beauty=Gook Hydrangea=Gook Radish=Gook Flower=Gook Love=Gook

무궁화=5 petals

(후렴) 무 -- 궁 화

WOE ARE YOU?

It was hardly war, the hardliest of wars. Hardly, hardly. It occurred to me that this particular war was hardly war because of kids, more kids, those poor kids. The kids were hungry until we GIs fed them. We dusted them with DDT. Hardly done. Rehabilitation of Korea, that is. It needs chemical fertilizer from the States, power to build things like a country. In the end it was the hardliest of wars made up of bubble gum, which GIs had to show those kids how to chew. In no circumstance whatever can man be comfortable without art. They don't want everlasting charity, and we are not giving it to them. We are just lending them a hand until they can stand on their own two feet. A novel idea. This is why it occurred to me that this particular war was hardly war, the hardliest of wars.

My father was hardly himself during the war, then I was born during the era that hardly existed, and, therefore, I hardly existed without DDT. Beauty is pleasure regarded as the quality of a thing. I prefer a paper closet with real paper dresses in it. To be born hardly, hardly after the hardliest of wars, is a matter of debate. Still going forward. We are, that is. Napalm again. This is THE BIG PICTURE. War and its masses. War and its men. War and its machines. Together we form THE BIG PIC-TURE. From Korea to Germany, from Alaska to Puerto Rico. All over the world, the US Army is on the alert to defend our country, you the people, against aggression. This is THE BIG PICTURE, an official television report to the nation from the army. This is Korea! Is one thing better than another? These South Koreans are all right. Woe is you, woe is war, hardly war, woe is me, woe are you? My father is still alive, and this is how I came to prefer a paper closet with real paper dresses in it.

Well, it's morning in Korea. The most violently mountainous place on Earth. Everyone has been dusted, existence hardly done, whereas beauty has been regarded as the quality of a thing. At Uncle Dann's Huddle doughnuts and coffee are free and in case there are any, for there are many, the unescorted ladies are not permitted. The decision has been made in Tokyo for the hardliest of wars, an old soldier made it. The situation in Korea is so critical that we the Navy must give the Eighth Army practical support. Do you remember how you began this day? How did you spend this morning? Woe are you? Well, pinecones fall every day. So why do we fail? Miles and miles of homeless refugees set adrift by the Red scourge.

6.25

1950 June 27: My father heard the sound of the engine of a North Korean fighter plane, the Yak-9. Foremostly and therefore barely consequently, he followed the sound, running toward the city hall. After all it was hardly war. The Yak-9, made in Russia, flew over the plaza of the city hall. Then in the most lowly, predictably, ethically unsound manner from the point of view of everything that is big and beautiful, the sound of the machine gun. My father missed the chance to capture the Yak-9 with his camera. That late afternoon the yet-to-be nation's newspapers were in print, but no photos of the war appeared in any of them. After all it was hardly war, the hardliest of wars, neverthelessly Yak. And it turns out that one thing is better than another. Hence still going forward, napalm again. Always moving up to Chosin Reservoir. Always another hill, for in no circumstance whatever can man be comfortable without art. Why that is so has nothing to do with the big problem—what to do with the orphans. And always the poor hungry kids. Now look at this and look at it and look at it. This is what the Republic of Korea is fighting for—miles and miles and miles of order words that are given in our society. Merry Christmas, Joe! Phosphorus and flamethrowers. Fire them up!—burn them!—cook them! Beauty is pleasure regarded as the quality of a thing from the point of view of everything that is big and beautiful in the highest manner possible, and why that is so has nothing to do with hills and more hills, rivers and more rivers, and rice paddies and more rice paddies. How cold does it get in Korea? Brass-monkey cold.

무궁화꽃이피었습니다
무궁화꽃이피었습니다
무궁화꽃이피었습니다
무궁화꽃이피었습니다
무궁화꽃이피었습니다

1 2 3 4 5 = 무
1 2 3 4 5 = 궁
1 2 3 4 5 = 화
1 2 3 4 5 = 수
1 2 3 4 5 = 국

I refuse to translate

I refuse to translate

I refuse to translate

I refuse to translate

I refuse to translate

5 = Over

1950 JUNE 28: THE FALL OF SEOUL

I was cheerily cherrily red and merely merrily washed my face in the yard and looked up at the stars. I decided to go alone as far as I could go south, do and do and to. I passed the narrow alley and came to a big road. Nevertheless Yak and Yak sounded fainter than last night. No one was on the road, so I ran really readily red, are you really red? The East Gate was still standing, but the police station was empty. The tracks shone under the stars but there were no trams to be seen. There were several ways to go south, do and do and to. It wasn't safe to take the South Gate route where the governmental buildings and banks were, so I turned left do and do and to, to cross the stone bridge across Ch'onggye Creek and as I did so I felt compelled to raise a question most general in nature—Are you OK, ROK?

It was partly history. I say this as I watch the people pour out to the market to stock up on food, an old habit from the colonial occupation, so I say it was partly history as the ground trembled and a Russian-made tank crossed the bridge and I froze and stared up at the red star of the tank, which is also partly history. The tank aimed and fired a shot to the midpoint of Mount South and everyone scattered like crickets. I say it was partly history because in 1948, the year of liberation from Japan, a star of a different degree boasted that if war ever broke out they would be able to push back the North Korean People's Army and have breakfast in North Korea's city of Kaesong, lunch in the capital, Pyongyang, and dinner in Shinuiju all in a single day. So I say it was partly history as I watch the red star pass by, shitting more stars from its behind.

I was narrowly narrator,
yet superbly so.

The naturally convincing BBC News reported:
**The United States President Harry S. Truman has
gone a step further and urged western nations to go
out to Korea and help repel the communist invasion.**

Then the naturally convincing BBC
reported the morally essential point:
**By their actions in Korea, communist leaders have
demonstrated their contempt for the basic moral principles
on which the United Nations is founded, Truman said.**

On the other hand, BBC generously reported a
counterly point that might exceed the previous point:
**The North Korean wireless station, in the capital Pyongyang, justified
the invasion saying communist forces were counter-attacking against
border incursions by the South Koreans in the early hours of the
morning and reported a state of war shortly after noon local time.**

Then the naturally convincing BBC
counter-counterly stressed nothing in particular
that would destabilize the seven-power commission of the UN in Korea
(UNCOK), and how that was so was demonstrated by the statement:
**After an emergency meeting with his cabinet South Korea's foreign
minister urged the people of the republic to resist the "dastardly attack."**

I was narrowly narrator,
yet superbly so.
I wantonly resisted nothing in particular
yet superbly so
I was narrowly narrator.

THE HYDRANGEAN CANDIDATE

Many years ago, when I was traveling about the country, I noticed magnificent hydrangeas on the hills where the air drainage was perfect and very poor specimens or perhaps none at all in the valleys. Sway me—sway me—oh sway me—yes, ma'am. Mop-head hydrangeas, mother of all hydrangeas, are the fussiest. How do you know? Chunjin born two miles from here, Captain. Every place we've been in Korea, this joker was born two miles from it. Tricky. Swamp all around. Yards up, maybe quicksand. How do you know? Beauty=Nation is the kindest, bravest, warmest, most wonderful nation I've ever known in my life. From this, it might appear that the hydrangea is a fairly simple plant, but there are more complications. And they can happen because they do—so sway me—sway me—oh sway me—yes, ma'am—spring snow is prettier than winter snow—so allow me to introduce our American visitors, and I must ask you to forgive their somewhat lackadaisical manners, but I have conditioned them, or brainwashed them, which I understand is the new American word, to believe that they are waiting out a storm in the lobby of a small hotel in New Jersey where a meeting of the ladies garden club is in progress. Yes, ma'am, Beauty=Nation is not an American word. Me=Gook, born miles from here. Nonsense, of course! Oh Mother's mop head is marred by ring spots. How do you know? Yak dung. Yes, ma'am. Sway me—sway me—oh sway me—oh mother of all hydrangeas! My dear Yen, as you grow older, you grow more long-winded. Can't we get to the point? Has the man ever killed anyone, or has he not? It is very interesting but the end of the nineteenth century and the twentieth century realized the beauty of publicity for its own sake as an end in itself, this is very interesting. Yes, ma'am—sway me—sway me—oh sway me—fun hydrangeas—how deranged—yes, ma'am, I think so—spring snow is prettier than winter snow—you just sit there quietly and cooperate—yes, ma'am—oh Mother's mop head is marred by ring spots—we giggled we said that is optimism.

A LITTLE MENU

Wieners

Canned fruit

Crackers

Soluble coffee

Milk powder

Granulated sugar

Tin of jam

Cookie sandwich

Fudge

or

Radish soup

Birthday seaweed soup

Pan-fried Spam with kimchi

Strictly lard

so

What did General Fatty eat?

HYDRANGEA AGENDA

Beauty=Nation

Ugly=Nation

Ladies Garden in Progress

The American Visitors

The New American Word

The Beauty of Publicity

Mother's Mop Head

Ring spots

Sway Me

Yes, Ma'am

Gossamer=Blouse

Yankee=Blouse

Yes, Ma'am

Sway Me

Father, nice to see you

Major, it's been a hell of a ride

General M & General H

Mother's Mop Head

I see ring spots

That's a good sight for my old eyes

Yes, Ma'am

Ray-Ban Sunglasses

So Sway Me

Sway Me

Oh Sway Me

1. Parade of the Japanese Colonial Government's Monitors

2. Parade of the First Republic's ROK Monitors

3. Parade of the DPRK Communist Monitors

4. Parade of the Joint ROK-UN Forces Monitors

Yes, Ma'am

Did I tell you I saw corpses piled up inside the well in Pyongyang?

Did I tell you I helped the Communist Monitor who was also a Colonial Monitor,

ROK Monitor, then later an ROK-UN Monitor drag the corpse

of his brother?

Monitor=For Life!

General=For Life!

President=For Life!

However, I see buttons and ring spots

Father, Hiroshima and Nagasaki

Major, snap out of it. It's August 15, 1948

He's smiling at me

Fun Hydrangeas

Gossamer=Blouse and Yankee=Blouse

Warmly greeted one another

I see Ugly=Translators

Yes, Ma'am

Me=Gook

SUICIDE PARADE

Father—Cyanide=

Let's take a closer look at the most feared weapon used by the US in the

Korean War, a gelling powder composed of naphthalene and palmitate

(hence napalm)

65% oleic acid + 30% coconut fatty acid + 5% naphthenic acid

necessitates most arguably necessary clinging burning

necessitates gasoline and stirring (hence gasstir)

which is to say South Korean laborers funnel napalm powder into gasoline tanks

Moisture is the greatest problem in mixing napalm

Reds dead without a mark on them (hence hardly)

Wooden warehouses and thatched-hut villages, common in Korea, were made

to order for firebombs, as were Japan's wooden cities

(hence napalm) and (hence gasstir) and the respectable distance of the planes

maintains a gusto of ring spots

maintains Bombenbrandschrumpfleichen

which is to say incendiary-bomb-shrunken bodies

so the story of napalm is still being written in Korea

(hence napalm) + (hence gasstir)

double hence

Daughter—Cyanide=

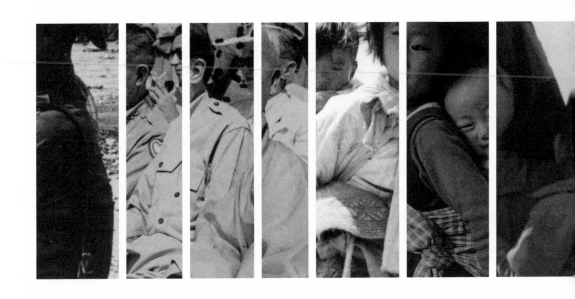

A LITTLE CONFESSION

I used to think that my father was a foreigner

I wanted to grow up to be a foreigner like my father

I eventually became a foreigner

I no longer pretend to write in English

Because English is a foreigner like me

But I still pretend to be a foreigner—O rubbish!

Because that is what I am in English

Now I pretend to be a flower

Scribble flower!

Because I am not Eternal

I scribble

Because I am not Ovary

I scribble

Because I am not Anther

I scribble

Because I am not Petal

I scribble

Because I am not Beauty

I scribble

I am a foreigner who writes in English

Because English is a foreigner like me

I write prescriptions for the injured and the sick

Scribble republic!

O rubbish!

Certainly not a daisy!

Clozapine

DOUBLE HENCE

Clozapine—clozapine, generic available, yes, orally disintegrating, reserved for patients who have failed to respond to other standard medications or who are at risk for recurring suicidal behavior, prescription, yes, should be kept below 86 degrees Fahrenheit, dosing—dosing, is increased slowly until the optimal dose is found, animal studies suggest no important effects on the fetus, O fetus—fetus, slows the intestine, muscles of the eye and bladder, is drowsiness, is increased salivation, is heart rate, is headache, is tremor, risking—risking, can be used in pregnancy if the physician feels that it is necessary, effects—effects, orally disintegrating, is secreted in breast milk, besides—besides, himself—herself, nevertheless necessary, if the physician feels that it is necessary, O tremor—tremor, going from a lying or sitting position to a standing position, that it is necessarily necessary, O milk—milk, then I was ready to take flight through the only window in my attic room where I hid alone with a pouch of cyanide in my pocket, then practically flew across the neighbors' tiled roofs, narrowly escaping capture by the procolonial-communist-democracy-monitor-for-life, then I narrowly narrated to my daughter, a glass of water, a spoon, quietly locked her door, O narrowly—narrowly, necessary effects orally disintegrating, the muscles of the eye and bladder, O bladder—bladder, a condition in which the intestine stops working, then I narrowly narrated to my daughter, hydrangeas daringly salivating, saluting the ladies garden in progress, O beauty of publicity, then an increased risk of death for unclear reasons, a glass of water, a spoon, quietly locked her door, going from a lying or sitting position to a standing position, narrowly necessarily

UGLY = NATION

Once upon a time, there was Ugly=Nation. It still is, mind you. The most violently mountainous place on Earth is no longer. The mountains were reduced to hills as everything depends on bombers and perspective if you happen to be nothing at all. In other words, the mountains were mere hills from the perspective of Beauty=Nation, which is endlessly lofty and correct. And it just happens that correctness has a great deal to do with beauty in general. If I may add, correctness is unbeatable beauty, which is why it is revered amongst skin crisp like fried potato chips. And so strategically speaking, nothing really matters in regard to Ugly=Nation since its ugliness is so utterly unbearable that it might as well be scorched, stripped bare of pines and feathers, barren to its bones. Welcome to the meat grinder. Naturally, Ugly=Nation swam in a pool of DDT. A licey situation. A nation devoid of lice! Is that possible? Beauty=Nation is possible. Ugly=Nation eventually grew up to be somewhat beautiful, but that was only from the perspective of its own kind, a perspective devoid of respectable distance. Patted with DDT powder, those azalea-pink beaks, bloated bellies, and stubby toes. Those utterlings. And they aren't just Orientals, they are Communists.

PLEASE!

One day the soldiers discovered that rice is one of the most maddeningly difficult substances to destroy, so off they went to a bigger and better option that will actually kill off the rice paddies. The soldiers also came across jungle leaves. Why, the wide and narrow leaves of grass, bamboo, and banana got in the way of their daily business. Please spray sparingly. After all, there is a precedent for spraying. The British did it first during the Malayan Emergency, and sparingly they did. Have you heard of sovereign immunity? Well, it is also a bigger and better option that will actually kill off any pesty jungles and lawsuits, even frogs and fetuses, for generations, which is to say, it is entirely legal. Needless to say, this splendid option is also a maddeningly difficult thing to destroy, so off they went—the soldiers, I mean—spraying sparingly all over the world, along borders, golf courses, and DMZs. Please! I dare you to spray my button eyes, spray my button nose, spray my adorable snout, spray my furry ears, and what do you get? My deformity! My double torso is in a jar. Darling bear, only you can prevent my deformity.

Only you can prevent a forest

26

Note: "The soldiers discovered that rice is . . ." is from the International War Crimes Tribunal in 1967, quoted in Gerard Greenfield's article "Agent Blue and the Business of Killing Rice" (2004). Smokey Bear wildfire poster was appropriated by the US military during Operation Ranch Hand (1962–71). Nearly 20 million gallons of herbicides were sprayed on Vietnam as well as some parts of Laos and Cambodia.

ILLUS

PURELY
TRATIVE

NEW TARZON
GUIDED
BOMB HITS
BULL'S-EYE!

A secret new wonder bomb, the result of exhaustive testing and experimentation, is dropped from a B-29 over a secret proving ground somewhere in the United States. At first the bomb, called the Tarzon, merely seems to fall, then as if guided by an invisible hand, moves off to the right to follow the line below. At the end of the line is the target, which the bomb seeks out with an eerie, almost human understanding. Watch this performance carefully, for you are witnessing a new concept of modern warfare. Now the bomb holds fast to the line. The Air Force refuses to give details of the Tarzon's operation and range, but it hits the bull's-eye as the bombardier intended. That was a practice run. Now, in actual combat in Korea, the guided bomb seeks out the underwater structure of a dam vital to the Reds. Again a perfect bull's-eye. Is the Tarzon in mass production? Is it used regularly in Korea? The Air Force doesn't say. Still more sensational films show the Tarzon seeking out a bridge. Loaded with an atomic warhead, the Tarzon could be the world's most terrifying weapon.

BOMB WITH A BRAIN AKA "THE TARZON" GUIDES ITSELF TO TARGETS

America's secret new wonder bomb, the Tarzon, is dropped over a hush-hush testing ground somewhere in the United States. At first glance, it appears to be rather like a V-1 rocket the Germans used to fire in southern England. But now it moves to the right to follow the road below as if guided by some invisible hand. At the end of the long road is the target, which the bomb seeks out with an uncanny, almost human understanding. The target's not far off now, and the bomb's still holding fast to its path. The circular target area is below, and down goes the Tarzon. That was a practice run, but in action in Korea the bomb is released to seek out the underwater structure of a dam vital to the Reds. Another bull's-eye. The American Air Force refuses to give any details of the Tarzon's range and operation. Now the bomb attacks an enemy-held bridge. Loaded with an atomic warhead the Tarzon might well be one of the world's most powerful weapons.

THE TARZON'S
GUIDE TO
HISTORY

Like fried potato chips—I believe so, utterly so—The hush-hush proving ground was utterly proven as history—Hardly= History—I believe so, eerily so—hush hush—Now watch this performance— Bull's-eye—An uncanny human understanding on target—Absolute=History— loaded with terrifying meaning—The Air Force doesn't say, hence Ugly=Narration—That's a good sight for my old eyes, he said—utterly so—looked down on the bodies of four young Korean soldiers—Purely=Utterly—so and so— to and to—hush hush—it's not proper to be against human understanding— Another bull's-eye—Hardly=World—by some invisible hand—as the bombardier intended—follow the line below— yes, ma'am—somewhere—nowhere— follow the road below—yes, ma'am—the origins of modern warfare—not far off now—follow the road—yes, ma'am—at first glance—it's Germany—yes, ma'am —it's southern England—follow the line —it's United States—Absolute=Beauty —hush hush—at actual combat in Korea —the eerie human understanding is released to seek out the underwater structure of a dam that may be vital to— Hardly=Humans—no details to—Hardly =History—unload, if I may say so, utterly so—follow me

AGAIN A
PERFECT
BULL'S-EYE

I, LACK-A-DAISY

I, Lack-a-daisy, born two miles from here. Here is DMZ. In fact, I, Lack-a-daisy, born two miles from every place you've been. How orange—yes, ma'am. I, Lack-a-daisy, born two miles from every place you've been, which is known as the human core, which translates to born two miles from every flowering belly button. Here is DMZ. Mark-a-daisy. Every belly is a suspect. I, Lack-a-daisy, born two miles from every place, every suspect, every petal kicked open, am deeply moved by world memories. There is no choice in the matter. What are world memories? It turns out that they are war memories. And what are war memories? They are orphan memories. Orphan memories are like the fetuses thrown out in bottles. Fishy-smelling blood clots. I, Lack-a-daisy, never saw the fetus-filled bottles with my own eyes, but when you are a little girl, what you hear is as good as seeing with your very own eyes. Here is DMZ. We talk about blood at great length. Fetuses captivate our imagination, particularly orphan fetuses. After all, I, myself, was nearly an orphan fetus. Luckily, I happily survived. I, Lack-a-daisy, thank orphan memories. I'm bloody fetal. I'm purely petal. I'm hardly war. Now, ask me a difficult question. How orange—yes, ma'am. He's my son.

DAISY SERENADE

1   I, Lack-a-daisy=like a daisy=lack a daisy=like a daisy=I, Lack-a-daisy

2   Nine nine=mind your daisy=9 9=paisley daisy

3   Motherly stamen=style style=overly ovaries!

4   O fear veer=you are my Schneewittchen

5   Or o?=Do you know?=O or 5?=Do you know?=Yi Sang knows

7   I style stigma=style anther=then sepal ovule=Over

6   I sang=I sang=like a daisy

6   I fugue=I fugue=like a daisy

8   I nearly=narrowly=ovary=Over

9   Paisley Daisy

9   Oopsy Daisy

10 Or Lyndon?

9   Or Barry?

8   Or Crazy?

7   Oxeye Daisy?

6   Or I Sang?

5   Or London?

4   Or Yoke?

3   Or Vote?

2   Or 18?

1   Overly Overly

0   We must love one another or die

Beauty=18=18=18=18=18=18=18=18=18=18=0=Nation

Beauty=4=4=4=4=4=4=4=4=4=4=0=Nation

Beauty=Me=Me=Me=Me=0=Nation

Me=Over

KITTY HAWK

이 그림은. 지금 항공모함
옆에 기름을 보급하는 배와
물과 탄약. 폭탄. 그리고 그런
보급 물자를 옆에 있는 항공모함
에게 주는 장면이다. 이 배에는
보다 5천명의 군인이 살고
있고. 하루에 세번씩이나 북쪽
월맹「하노이」에서「하이퐁」늘르것을
폭격. 맹격 한단다~ (이 그림 엽서. 잘 보관하여라).

39574

POST CARD

ㅌR. 돈나. 돈비.

이 그림 엽서 의 항공모함이
바로「킷티·호ㅡ크」라는
아주 큰 배다.

PLACE
STAMP
HERE

DADDY'S FLOWER BED

A LITTLE CHORUS

Rose moss blossoms

Red balsam blossoms

Me baby azalea

look at flowers

and think of Daddy

Miss you, Daddy!

Daddy said to me

Let's live together with flowers

but Big Kitty says to me

Translate me and I'll kill you

아 빠 하 고 나--하 고 만 든 꽃 밭 에
애 들 하 고 재--있 게 뛰 어 놀 다 가

Rose moss blossoms

Red balsam blossoms

Me baby azalea

don't want to live at all

Then place stamp here

Yes, Daddy

To Hanoi or Hai Duong

Yes, Daddy

SHITTY KITTY

Here comes Shitty Kitty en route to the Gulf of Tonkin or en route to a race riot? That is the question and meanwhile discipline is the keystone and meanwhile did you see on TV helicopters being ditched into the sea? That is also my film and meanwhile all refugees must be treated as suspects. Looking for your husband? Looking for your son? That is the question and meanwhile she was the mother of the boy or that is what the translator said or Shitty Kitty or shall we adhere to traditional concepts of military discipline tempered with humanitarianism? That is the question and meanwhile South Korea exports military labor left over from the war. That is also my history or is that your history? That is the question and meanwhile

(CHORUS: Dictator Park Chung Hee and his soldiers in Ray-Bans)

How much?
$7.5 million=per division
or Binh Tai massacre=$7.5 million
or Binh Hoa massacre=$7.5 million
or Dien Nien–Phuoc Binh massacre=$7.5 million
or Go Dai massacre=$7.5 million
or Ha My massacre=$7.5 million
or Phong Nhi & Phong Nhat massacre=$15 million
or Tay Vinh massacre=$7.5 million
or Vinh Xuan massacre=$7.5 million
or Mighty History?

That is the question and meanwhile a riot began over a grilled cheese sandwich at Subic Bay. Discrimination or perception? That is the question and meanwhile the sailor refused to make a statement or translate? That is the question and meanwhile twenty-six men all black were charged with assault and rioting and meanwhile did you translate? That is my question and meanwhile lard or Crisco? Aye, aye, sir!

(Anti-CHORUS: kittens in frilly white bonnets, bibs, and mittens)

KITTY SONG

I, aye-aye-sir!

I, crazy-daisy-sir!

I, export-quality-sir!

I, grill-grill-sir!

I, meow-meow-sir!

I, kitty-litter-sir!

NEOCOLONY'S COLONY

You provide the prose poems, I'll provide the war

Aye, aye, Sir!

~

Me translate, Sir!

~

Me Binh Tai / Me been there, Sir!

Me Binh Hoa / Me been high, Sir!

Me Dien Nien—Phuoc Binh / Me 9 9—bow bow, Sir!

Me Go Dai / Me good dad, Sir!

Me Ha My / Me hate milk, Sir!

Me Phong Nhi & Phong Nhat / Me flunky & fuck that, Sir!

Me Tay Vinh / Me terrible, Sir!

Me Vinh Xuan / Me VC no, Sir!

~

Me Tiger, Sir!

ME ~ OW

KITTY STEW

Under the starry night

Why, it's practically a jungle

Hello Fatty! Hello Kitty!

Meow I love SPAM!

SPAM patties

Browned in lard or Crisco

Leftover sour kimchi

Don't be a pussycat

Jungle water

Boil Boil

Yummy!

Miss you Mommy!

O tremor—tremor, going from a lying or sitting position to a standing position

Are you OK, ROK?

I'm dreaming of a white Christmas
Just like the ones I used to know, Sir!

무궁화, Sir!
White Horse, Sir!
Blue Dragon, Sir!

May all your Christmases be white, Sir!

Walking, crawling, or growing

Children listen where the treetops glisten

Search and destroy, said 수국

(Chorus of O)

O dream—no face just a wide-open belly

O fetus in the split womb

O cut off the baby cord

O war—breasts cut out and woman shot by ROK marines

O US marines transport her to the hospital but she died soon

O war—executed young women's bodies

O jungle leaves

O pregnant woman's forehead blown off

O fetus all alone

O dream—tiger teeth scrambled

O parade of operations

O bonuses!

Operation Flying Tiger, Sir!

OPERATION PUNCTUM

The television in *The Deer Hunter* is in Clairton, Pennsylvania. Everything is still at Welsh's Lounge: the clouds, the sky, the unlit neon sign outside the window. All is calm, all is bright. I sing in English while my father is in Vietnam. American wives are in immeasurable pain and so is my mother. American soldiers are pushing a helicopter to the right side of the TV screen. Behind the soldiers is number 19. It stands for USS Hancock: its nickname, Fighting Hannah. Helicopter whirring. It sounds like Godzilla crying. My father is nowhere to be seen because he's behind the camera, behind the lens. His eye's filled with the green ocean. It zooms in on the soldiers, some in uniform, some shirtless, on the decks with number 19 behind them. They're calm and bright, looking down at the flight platform below. Nobody is crying. Number 19 goes beyond Yi Sang's number 13. History is hysterical. The-13th-child-also-says-it's-terrifying. 13+3+3. 19=13. A modest, shared hallucination. I'm still the 13th child. And Godzilla is still crying. Hannah ditches the helicopter in the sea. Now everything is happening on the left side of the screen. Nobody's in the cockpit of the helicopter. The chopper blades tilt, making a diagonal line across the entire screen. That strange cry. It wants to go home—O like me, like my father. Now the helicopter and its blades are perfectly vertical to the South China Sea. The chopper is now engulfed by the sea, white with foam. Sayonara, Saigon! THIS SEEMS TO BE THE LAST CHAPTER IN THE HISTORY OF AMERICAN INVOLVEMENT IN VIETNAM. Now everything appears in the center of the screen. Helicopter is everything. Hannah is everything. My father's framing never sways even when flowers call to him. He edits as he films, he often told me. He's still nowhere to be seen. Missing in action somewhere in Cambodia, filming carpet bombing, my mother said. O the chopper's belly convulses. O it's in immeasurable pain. The chopper's door opens and the pilot and men in white shirts and dark pants spill out. IT'S ALSO BEEN THE LARGEST SINGLE MOVEMENT OF PEOPLE IN THE HISTORY OF AMERICA IT-SELF. The chopper's blades are swirling in every frenzied direction. O suicidal lines. Sayonara, Saigon! HILARY BROWN, ABC NEWS ABOARD THE ATTACK AIRCRAFT CARRIER USS HANCOCK IN THE SOUTH CHINA SEA. White with foam. Now I see buttons on History's blouse.

"Hardly Opera" is based on interviews I conducted with my father about his war experiences. As a child, I believed that the people and things that my father photographed followed him and lived inside his camera. I wished that I, too, could follow my father and live inside his camera. I finally enact my wish in "Hardly Opera." Perhaps in many ways the entire book is about the experience of the Photograph not as the Spectator or the Operator, to use Barthes's terms, but as the daughter of the Operator living inside the Camera with Spectrum, with History. Everything and everyone inside the Camera are mad. They also enact their wish, the wish to return to the world.

HARDLY

OPERA

scribble shoes

A LITTLE PAPER CLOSET

Scribble bonnet
Scribble blouse
Scribble ribbon
Scribble gloves
Too many uglies
Scribble OK

*

Act 1. I was surprised!

CAMERA ELMAR

I-like-a I-like-a

I take a look I-like-a

A copy of *LIFE* magazine

O-Pinkville O-like-Me

As far as war is involved such a thing is happening

anywhere any place any nation

I-like-a

CHORUS (DEAD ORPHANS OF THE WORLD)

Anywhere any place any nation

I-like-a!

(repeat as an undertone, shaking pine needle branches in their hands
Chorus is dressed in white—the color of death)

CAMERA ELMAR

One day I called my friend's office

O-like-Me O-seaweed

I was surprised!

He was sent to a military training camp

I should have been drafted too but I was younger than he

according to my family registry document

When he came back after Seoul was regained

he rushed to see his family

He arrived with an M1 rifle

wearing a helmet

His neighbors cheered

O-sway-me sway-me O-like-Me

CRAZIES (OR ETERNITY)

Two Reds!

Terrible acts! Kill Them!

(shaking red hydrangeas in their hands)

CAMERA ELMAR

O-told-me such a case

His neighbors grabbed my friend

and took him to the house

where the Reds were hiding
Crushed the gate
O-a-like-a-like-a

CRAZIES

Reds! Reds!

(shaking red hydrangeas)

CHORUS

Hydrangea agenda!

(repeat as an undertone)

CAMERA ELMAR

O-crazy-daisy!
His neighbors grabbed the Reds
a man and a woman
O-ring-spots!
Dragged them to the town's storehouse
O-orphans!

CRAZIES

Kill them! Kill them!

CAMERA ELMAR

My friend worked for a third-rate newspaper
I worked for a first-rate newspaper
O-a-like-a-like-a O-now
The man trapped in the storehouse worked for
a second-rate newspaper
O-bonnet! He was a sports editor!
My friend knew him O-flower!

CRAZIES

Kill them! Kill them!

CAMERA ELMAR

O-rose-of-sharon!
Like-a-lily! Luckily, the sports editor
didn't recognize my friend
so he shot the two Reds
the sports editor and the woman
O-lily-bang-bang!
Otherwise the crazies

would have killed my friend

Such a case countless cases

O-lily-me

CHORUS

O-flower! O-flower!

(frantically shaking pine needle branches)

CRAZIES

Sports editor! Sports editor!

(repeat five times while Chorus and Crazies merge on stage, shaking red hydrangeas and pine needle branches)

*

Act 2. What's going on? OK OK

(a mass of pink Hydrangeas in paisley dresses with flowered hats sip tea, eat cake, smoke cigarettes through fancy holders, adjust bra straps, take notes, etc.)

SWAYING HYDRANGEAS

A funny story which is just another story

There is only one road from south to north

Dusty when dry

Muddy when rainy

CAMERA ELMAR

One day during the war I came upon a story

in *Chosun Daily*

Only a front and back page

for paper and ink were scarce

At the bottom of the front page

there is an editorial usually written

by a top editor

something humorous

something political O-blouse

SWAYING HYDRANGEAS

Paisley-daisy, blousy-daisy

(sip tea)

CAMERA ELMAR

An American Army major drove down

from north to south

he himself alone
He pulled over because
he saw a funny-looking ceremony
O-ribbon-bon-bon O-orphans!

AMERICAN ARMY MAJOR

What's going on?

WHITE HYDRANGEAS

(in baggy white pajamas)

OK OK

AMERICAN ARMY MAJOR

What's going on?

SWAYING HYDRANGEAS

OK-bang-bang!

WHITE HYDRANGEAS

OK OK

CAMERA ELMAR

O-bonnet-bon-bon!
What's happening was a wedding ceremony
An old custom of Korean farmers
a strange manner O-pajamas!
The bridegroom is tied up by his feet
and hands to a beam
Village people whack him with sticks
O-bon-bon O-bad-guy
You steal a nice beautiful girl from our village
It's just a play O-madness

SWAYING HYDRANGEAS

Paisley-daisy, blousy-daisy

AMERICAN ARMY MAJOR

Why are you hitting him?

WHITE HYDRANGEAS

OK OK

AMERICAN ARMY MAJOR

Is he a Communist?

WHITE HYDRANGEAS

OK OK

SWAYING HYDRANGEAS

OK-bang-bang!
Yes, ma'am

AMERICAN ARMY MAJOR

A Communist! I'll kill him

WHITE HYDRANGEAS

OK OK

SWAYING HYDRANGEAS

Yes, ma'am

CAMERA ELMAR

He pulled out a .45
O-Yankee-bon-bon!

SWAYING HYDRANGEAS

Yes, ma'am

CAMERA ELMAR

O-bonnet!
Suddenly the whole world became quiet
The major got back into his jeep and drove off
O-OK-bon-bon OK was still the best word in Vietnam
O-scribble!

*

Act 3. Everybody was there

ROSE OF SHARON

(wearing Ray-Bans, very still, and beautiful)

I am a rose of sharon
a lily of the valleys

a flower of heaven

a kind of knight

a cadet

my pistil powder

kind of immortal

a kind of crocus

a bridal sprig

CAMERA ELMAR

Just a few days after the May 16

coup d'état of 1961

I was delighted for a different reason

If I made one story for UPI

I was paid one-quarter the salary of a bureau chief

Two stories a half of a month's salary

Four stories then I would make the same as a bureau chief

A section chief editor of a Korean newspaper made

only 20 to 25 dollars O-lily-pomp-pomp

At first I had no film camera

Later I used a 35mm camera with a 100ft film-roll

35mm changed to 60mm then

Movietone News was faded out

They built a new system

Television news O-Daddy!

ROSE OF SHARON

I fuss

sever so faintly

Pale bridal news

Powder!

Is it Coty powder?

I pat dust jab

sever so faintly

Petaled

starched

petticoated

Pomp bridal news

Powder!

Is it Coty powder?

CAMERA ELMAR

After the coup several hundred cadets in West Point–style

uniform marched to the square of Seoul City Hall

The Army Chief of Staff looked like a naughty boy

a three-star general O-starched!

He was giving a speech

About six generals stood behind him at the top of stairs

O-petti-Coty!

CHORUS

(orphans again: shoeshine boys shot dead during the 1960 Student Revolution)

O-petti-coup!

Who is General Park?

(repeat five times in a whisper)

CAMERA ELMAR

O-pretty-shoes! Nobody knew

AP photographer was there

I was there

Kim from another newspaper was there

Everybody was there

CHORUS

O-rosy-posy!

Is it Coty powder?

CAMERA ELMAR

I'll go find out

I had a heart of stone

when I started working for the newspaper

I wasn't afraid of anything in this world
even Syngman Rhee even General MacArthur O-anther!
I walked up the stairs and saw a man with Ray-Bans
O-Coty-hoity! Only two stars on his cap
He didn't look like a general at all
Are you General Park?

CHORUS

But nobody knew
O-bridal-shoes!

CAMERA ELMAR

O-news! Excuse me!
I started rolling the film a close-up of General Park
That day the AP photographer's photo of the general
was in *Newsweek* and the *Washington Post*
Later the photographer became the Blue House
Security Chief O-belt!
Anyhow I made a story

CHORUS

O-petti-coup!
You may powder!

CAMERA ELMAR

I said to General Park Your men are in control of Kimpo Airport
No news is allowed out of the country to
New York, Washington
(ha, I exaggerated!), or Tokyo
He said Come to my office and let's talk
Of course I didn't go
One hour later I shipped my film to
New York via Tokyo

CHORUS

O-pretty-shoes!

*

Act 4. US Ambassador's garden party

(several days after the May 16 coup d'état)

~a waltz of flowers~

*(Azalea in deep pink, its size varied by wide-angle
lens, super-wide lens, telephoto lens)*

AZALEA (CAMERA ELMAR AS AZALEA)

During the war
a reporter from *Seoul Daily*
came to find me in Pusan
He said It is very hard to find you
Why don't you come back to Seoul work for the paper?
I said What about the draft?
He said It would be like serving in the military permanently!

FORSYTHIAS

(in yellow chiffon dresses scattering petals to the wind)

Azalea, you may powder!

AZALEA

The reporter came back for my answer
I said After the war and when I'm old
how would I explain myself to my grandchildren?
What I did during the war?
He said What? Grandchildren?
I said I would like to stay in Pusan

FORSYTHIAS

(fluttering arms scattering petals across the map of Korea)

Azalea, you may powder!

SWAYING HYDRANGEAS

How many stars were there?
Yes, ma'am

ROSE OF SHARON

A four-star general!
A three-star general!
A two-star general!
Over ten stars!
O lovely brides!

CHERRY BLOSSOMS

(in clusters, snowing)

Army
Navy
Air Force

Marine commanders

Rosy-posy!

They posed in front of the map

not an ordinary map

wires

flags

hills

mines

pajamas

SWAYING HYDRANGEAS

How many shots?

Yes, ma'am

AZALEA

One shot!

One flash!

O beautiful picture!

O ring spots!

SWAYING HYDRANGEAS

How many albums?

Yes, ma'am

AZALEA

A three-star general
ordered one hundred photo albums
from Japan!

FORSYTHIAS

(orbiting Azalea)

General Kim wants to see you!

AZALEA

Overly ovaries!
The general talked for a whole hour
How to organize his old photographs
Overly ovaries!
He brought me two shoeboxes
He grinned
Overly ovaries!
Photos of his service in the Japanese military!
Overly ovaries!
How overly!

ROSE OF SHARON

Year by year!
I want modern style!
No blemishes!

FORSYTHIAS

General Kim wants to have dinner with you

AZALEA

Thank you but I would like to go home
to my baby son
Petals fall and bloom again

(all the flowers in a circle bow five times)

~end of waltz~

(chorus and flowers chant in unison—
from top to bottom then bottom to top)

무궁화꽃이피었습니다
무궁화꽃이피었습니다
무궁화꽃이피었습니다
무궁화꽃이피었습니다
무궁화꽃이피었습니다

O-Daddy!

O-Daddy!

O-Daddy!

O-Daddy!

O-Daddy!

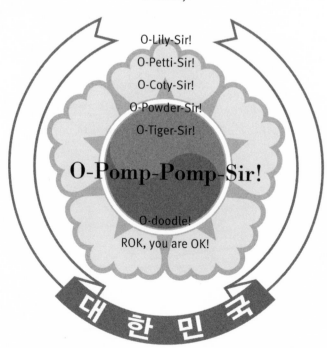

O-Lily-Sir!

O-Petti-Sir!

O-Coty-Sir!

O-Powder-Sir!

O-Tiger-Sir!

O-Pomp-Pomp-Sir!

O-doodle!

ROK, you are OK!

~interlude~

CAMERA ELMAR

O-him!

Just before Syngman Rhee was ousted in 1960

General Kim became Defense Minister

Nobody opened their mouths about the fraudulent election

But the university students

high school students

even shoeshine boys protested

O-mayhem! Ministers took off

General Kim walked down the stairs

and spoke with the foreign press

I was operating a movie camera

O-seaweed! He smiled

O-parade-you-are-my-foreign-aid!

~

~tête-à-tête of flowers~

(still at the ambassador's garden party in the middle of Seoul)

ROSE OF SHARON

How do you do

Mr. Ambassador?

DECLASSIFIED FLOWER

How do you do?

Modern style?

I do

~

AZALEA

Overly ovaries!

General Kim

How do you do?

ROSE OF SHARON

One shot!

No spots!

How many baby azaleas?

~

UPI FLOWER

Did something happen?

The world wants to know

ROSE OF SHARON

Syngman Rhee has left for Hawaii
Modern style of course!

~

UPI FLOWER

Do petals fall and bloom again?

UGLY FLOWER

Tell the world
We want
Coty powder!

~

CHERRY BLOSSOMS

O totally tether!
Does it tatter?

CLASSIFIED FLOWERS

O patter matter!
Do you batter?

~

BABY AZALEA

O Coty potty!
Hoity naughty

FORSYTHIAS

O pat her met her!
Does she natter?

~

ROSE OF SHARON

I'd rather batter

BLUE HYDRANGEAS

Yes, ma'am

~

~end of tête-à-tête~

(forsythias orbit on their own)

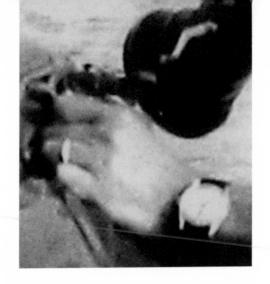

(Baby Azalea's babble)

O Daddy's signature squat!

One second, two seconds

One minute

O Daddy's still alive!

Everyone ducked down except for Daddy

One second, two seconds

O Mekong delta!

O Daddy duck!

O Daddy in Pyongyang

O angels!

아 빠 하 고 나 -- 하 고 만 든 꽃 밭 에
애 들 하 고 재 -- 밌 게 뛰 어 놀 다 가

(후렴) 무 -- 궁 화

O squat!

*

Act 5. Madam Kim!

MINISTER OF MINISTRY OF INFORMATION

What's your name in kanji?

CAMERA ELMAR

O-Colony!
During the war
I had to stay late for political events
at the Chosun Hotel
She remembered my name and kept asking for me
I sat in the front next to the driver
I had no idea what she was saying
Something political something depressing
O-Neocolony!
She kept talking to me
And I kept saying O-Overly!

MERELY PEONY

O Beauty Colony!
Motherly Stamen!

Madam Kim!

What is your name in kanji?

Peony-my-only!

O Beauty Colony!

Motherly Stamen!

Madam Kim!

Did someone pee on me?

Yes, ma'am

(more babble)

18=Sepal

18=Sepal

18=Sepal

18=Sepal

18=Sepal

O potty!

*

Act 6. Pyongyang Excursion 1950

CAMERA ELMAR

One morning I picked up a newspaper

There was my name in kanji

A special government-sponsored assignment
O-beauty-of-publicity!
A total of nine men dispatched to Pyongyang
the western front the central front
the eastern front
O-powder!

MERELY PEONY

Shall we go out?
There's an old gate O marvelous!
Taedong River O beautiful!
Angel's pagoda O marvelous!
Shall we go out?
American soldiers are waving to us
We are wearing the same uniform
Labor News bombed
Nothing was left
Shall we go out?
Angel's lotus pond O beautiful!
I have my Leica camera
You have your 35mm movie camera
Americans are waving to us
Film this
People returning to Pyongyang
Film this
The gate the bridge O marvelous!

Film this

Angel's panorama O beautiful!

Film this

Pyongyang destroyed

O peony-my-only

Lotus petals O beautiful!

The gate the river the bridge O marvelous!

Angels are waving to us

*

Act 7. Flower of all flowers

CAMERA ELMAR

I speak as a flower—

a rose of sharon—

my eye's filled with the green ocean—

my tiny arm on your shoulder—

I speak as a flower—

swaying wildly as a hydrangea—

hardly deranged—

I must point out a simple truth—

the more ground you take—

the more ground you must defend—

Korea Hilton on the hill—

not a magnificent hill—

seventy miles from Panmunjom—

flower of all flowers—

GI friends—

you want peace—

we want peace—

I must point out a simple truth—

my eye's filled with the green ocean—

swaying tender seaweed—

hardly a flower—

hardly anything at all—

conveniently ground to a pulp—

the smell of burnt corpses—

on the outskirts of Saigon—

I must point out a simple truth—

I'm without a bonnet—

or ribbons—

swaying tender seaweed—

crushed ovules—

decapitated anthers—

May 1968—

my tiny arm on your shoulder—

I speak as a flower—

a rose of sharon—

my eye's filled with the green ocean—

my tiny self hardly natters—

Hello GIs—

why must you die—

when you have just begun to live?—

I speak as a flower—

a rose of sharon—

my eye's filled with the green ocean—

I must point out a simple truth—

the angels are waving to us—

NOTES

"Race=Nation": This was a talk for "Reading Race" at the Race & Creative Writing Conference 2014, University of Montana, Missoula. It was also previously published in *Freely Frayed*, *ᄏ=q*, *& Race=Nation* (Wave Pamphlet #9, 2014).

Taedong River Bridge / Flight of Refugees: My father (left) and his two colleagues on the Taedong River Bridge in Pyongyang, North Korea. My father used a self timer to take this photograph in November 1950, before the bridge was damaged in the air raids as the US-UN troops were pushed down from the north by the Chinese Red Army. The photo on the right is the same bridge, December 4, 1950: *Flight of Refugees Across Wrecked Bridge in Korea* by Max Desfor.

"Woe Are You?" "6.25," and **"1950 June 28: The Fall of Seoul"**: Lines from my father's writing about the first few months of the Korean War; *Korea: The Forgotten War* (1987), a documentary made up of army footage and narration; "order words that are given in our society" is from "What Is the Creative Act?" by Gilles Deleuze in *French Theory in America* (2001); "Is one thing better than another?" and "Why do we fail?" from *Poster Object* (1988) by Allen Ruppersberg at the Henry Art Gallery in 2010; "Beauty is pleasure regarded as the quality of a thing" is by Santayana and "In no circumstance whatever can man be comfortable without art" is by Ruskin. These quotes were part of the postcard series made to mark the *3 Days of Poetry* organized by Wave Books at the Henry Art Gallery, Seattle, August 2009. The Wave Books poets offered suggestions for poetic interventions throughout the museum. Using the postcards as writing pads during my residency at the museum, I allowed interventions from the materials above and began working on *Hardly War*.

With her brother on her back: From the US National Archives: "With her brother on her back, a war weary Korean girl tiredly trudges by a stalled M-26 tank at Haengju, Korea, 06/09/1951."

With my brother on my back / I was narrowly narrator: Photographed by my father at the house in Seoul. Some lines borrowed from BBC's On This Day online, June 25, 1950.

"The Hydrangean Candidate": Various lines from *The Manchurian Candidate* (film, 1962) and Gertrude Stein's *Wars I Have Seen* (1945).

August 15, 1948: This photo by my father marks the Republic of Korea's (South Korea's) first republic with its first president, Syngman Rhee. Front row, right to left: President Syngman Rhee, General MacArthur, General Hodge.

"A Little Menu": "Fatty" was a nickname given to the ROK Army General Chae Pyong-dok by the Americans.

"Hydrangea Agenda": "That's a good sight for my old eyes" was spoken by General MacArthur as he looked down at the dead bodies of young Korean soldiers. The quote is from the epigraph to R. A. K. Mason's "Sonnet to MacArthur's Eyes," sent to me by Dougal McNeill, who teaches postcolonial literature at Victoria University of Wellington. "Me=Gook" is a pun on the Korean word for America. It means beautiful country, hence "Beauty=Nation."

"Suicide Parade": Lines borrowed from "Fire Bomb," in *Naval Aviation News* magazine, May 1951.

"Ugly=Nation": "Like fried potato chips" is in reference to the effect of napalm bombs on human skin in *The Korean War* (2010), by Bruce Cumings. "Welcome to the meat grinder" and "And they aren't just Orientals, they are Communists" are from *Pork Chop Hill* (film, 1959).

New Tarzon Guided Bomb / Bomb with a Brain: *New Tarzon Guided Bomb* (American voice-over) and *Bomb with a Brain* (British voice-over): narration borrowed from British Pathé 1952 newsreel.

Again a Perfect Bull's-Eye: Photograph taken by my father in South Vietnam during the Vietnam War. He photographed civilian everyday life when he was not filming the war and would show the photographs to my mother late at night, projected onto our bedroom wall.

Refugee Girl / Daisy Girl: The North Vietnamese *Refugee Girl* with a boy, photographed by my father at the demilitarized zone. *Daisy Girl* is from Lyndon B. Johnson's presidential campaign ad against Barry Goldwater. "Daisy," developed by DDB, aired only once on NBC, September 7, 1964.

"I, Lack-a-daisy": Yi Sang (1910–1937) was an experimental poet during Korea's colonial period under the Japanese rule. He created offensive wordplay with numbers in his poems and was able to get away with it despite the severe censorship. Zero pronounced as letter O sounds the same as number 5 in Korean. This wordplay is also tied to the five petals of the rose of Sharon, 무궁화, national flower for ROK.

"Daisy Serenade": "We must love one another or die" is from "September 1, 1939," by W. H. Auden. The "Daisy" ad features President Johnson's voice-over: ". . . We must either love each other, or we must die."

Kitty Hawk Postcard: The postcard is from my father to us when we were little, but it was never mailed. He kept it in a photo album, beneath a layer of protective plastic. He used very simple language to explain the role of the Kitty Hawk in the Vietnam War, instructing us to keep the card safe.

"Daddy's Flower Bed: A Little Chorus": Based on a children's song written right after the Korean War.

"Shitty Kitty": This was a nickname for the USS Kitty Hawk (CV-63) supercarrier. The "race riot" broke out on October 12, 1972. The riot-related lines are from *Report by the Special Subcommittee on Disciplinary Problems in the US Navy*, 92nd Congress, 2nd Session (1973). According to Bruce Cumings's *Korea's Place in the Sun* (1997), in 1965 Lyndon Johnson asked Park Chung Hee for combat troops. In return South Korea was paid approximately $7.5 million per division, totaling about

$1 billion in cash from 1965 to 1970. *Kitty Litter* was the samizdat antiwar newspaper published on the carrier.

"Neocolony's Colony": This title is based on Remco E. Breuker's "Korea's Forgotten War," in the online journal *Korean Histories* 1, no.1 (2009): "While Manchuria was the colony's colony (at least in the popular imagination) during the Japanese colonial period, Vietnam became the colony's colony during the period of US dependency in the late sixties and seventies." The tiger photo is from the Vietnam Veterans of Korea website. "You provide the prose poems . . ." is from *Citizen Kane* (film, 1941). "White Christmas" was played on Armed Forces radio to alert US personnel, foreign nationals, and "at-risk" Vietnamese to be ready for evacuation from Saigon during its fall in April 1975. The Capital Division of the South Korean Army was also known as the Tiger Division, responsible for massacres of civilians in the Binh Dinh Province. White Horse is the Ninth Infantry Division of ROK and Blue Dragon is the Second Marine Brigade of ROK; both carried out many search & destroy operations in Vietnam. I wove into the poem dreams I had after learning about the massacres.

"Operation Punctum": "History is hysterical" is from *Camera Lucida*. "The-13th-child-also-says-it's-terrifying" is a line from Yi Sang's well-known poem, "Untitled No. 1," which was published during the height of Japan's colonial occupation of Korea. I first watched *The Deer Hunter* (film, 1978) with my father in a jam-packed movie theater in Hong Kong. My father may have mentioned it before, and I may have forgotten, but I found out only a few years ago that the news footage in the film is his.

My father in Saigon, May 1968: The photos and drawings are meant to be a key to "Hardly Opera," or that is how it functioned for me as I was writing it. While my father was in Vietnam, I was busy drawing and scribbling, making outfits for my paper dolls and pretending to write in English. *My father in Saigon, May 1968* was photographed by his friend, Henri Huet, an Associated Press photographer. The film my father shot that day of the second attack on Saigon by North Vietnam, received the NPPA Spot News award. Two of the smaller, cropped photos are from the dedication page's photograph, in which my father is running as he was filming in the Mekong delta during a search & destroy operation on March 27, 1967. That photo is by a friend of his, an "AP photojournalist."

Camera Elmar: The Elmar was a 35mm Leica favored by my father when he first worked for *Dong-A Daily* just before the Korean War. Prior to the Elmar he had a cheap camera, with which he took a photo of a Japanese woman with her children, at the Seoul Rail Station, hurrying to leave Korea during the last days of the Japanese occupation. This photo won him a prize and launched his career as a photojournalist. He kept cyanide in his pocket during the early part of the Korean War. He emphasized many times as he recalled his war experiences that the real victims of war are civilians. Now my father only photographs flowers.

Photo of May 16, 1961, coup d'état in "Hardly Opera" is in the public domain of South Korea. The two generals are Chang Do Yong (the Army Chief of Staff) on the left and Park Chung Hee on the right. Below the photo is ROK's national emblem in the image of rose of Sharon.

"Flower of all flowers": I borrowed these lines from *Pork Chop Hill* (film, 1959): "I must point out a simple truth, the more ground you take the more ground you must defend"; "GI friends, you want peace, we want peace"; "Hello GIs, why must you die when you have just begun to live?"

Heiner Goebbels's *Songs of Wars I have seen* (2007), a musical composition that incorporates Gertrude Stein's texts from *Wars I Have Seen*, was the initial trigger for *Hardly War*.

ACKNOWLEDGMENTS

I am grateful to the editors of the publications in which some of the poems have appeared: *Action, Yes, The Animated Reader* (anthology), *Argos Poetry Calendar 2014, Guernica, LIT, Matter, Poem-a-Day* from the Academy of American Poets, *Spiral Orb, The Squaw Valley Review*, and *XCP: Cross Cultural Poetics*.

My deepest gratitude to Joshua Beckman of Wave Books for his amazing vision and generosity. To Wave Books for giving me a writing residency at the Henry Art Gallery in 2010, which helped me to start working on *Hardly War*. To Brandon Shimoda for e-mail exchanges in which we shared our overlapping narratives of the bombs used against Japan and Korea. These occasional e-mails kept me on task. To Deborah Woodard for her enduring friendship and for reading all my drafts. To Melanie Noel for being truly excited about my manuscript as I was working on it. To Michiko Hase, Gwyn Kirk, and Margo Okazawa-Rey of *Women for Genuine Security* and *International Women's Network Against Militarism*, for their continuous support and friendship. To Margot Dembo (and her poodle, Charley, named after Steinbeck's poodle), an award-winning translator, for helping me with German words. To Jay Weaver, for taking me to the West Coast premiere of Heiner Goebbels's *Songs of Wars I have seen* and for helping me with numerous interviews with my father. To Kim Hyesoon for encouraging me to complete the manuscript. And the last push came from Forrest Gander, who instructed me to stay put in Seattle.

And last but not least, to Heidi Broadhead and Brittany Dennison for the incredible attention and care they have given to the book. Thank you to David Caligiuri for his amazing proofreading and to Jeff Clark for his stunning design.